Poems from an Eclectic Mind

David D Plain

Trafford rev. 04/13/2016

 www.trafford.com
North America & international
toll-free: 1 888 232 4444 (USA & Canada)
fax: 812 355 4082

This work is dedicated to my wife
Gisele, especially the love poems.

CONTENTS

Love at First Voice

Anji's Phileo 3
Beauty 7
Death's Sudden Embrace 8
Love at First Voice 9
Love on the Doorstep 10
Love, Murder and Madness 11
Of Eros and Other Things 13
Places of the Heart 14
Seasons of Time 15

Bearer of Prayers

Apparition 19
Bearer of Prayers 21
Faith, Hope and Love 22
Immortality 23
Inside My Mother's Womb 25
Metamorphosis 27
Origins 28
Pain 29
Session on the Bench 30
The Windigo from Nepissing 31
Truth 33

Imagine a World

Thirteen Essential Literary Terms 37
Conundrum 38
Imagine A World 40
Of Quasars and Quarks 41

Gisele's Place

Aamjiwnaang 45
Gisele's Place 46
Ode to Canada 48
Rejuvenation 51
The Witch of November 52
Wihat, Tico and Bear 53

Rendezvous with an Ancestor

Cold Winter Chores 57
Dammit I'm Mad 59
Growing Old 60
Limericks in Honour of John 62
Remember the Raisin 63
Rendezvous with an Ancestor 66
Summer in the City 68
The Keys to the Kingdom 69
The Very Best Years 70
Wafting 72
Worm Pickers' Delight 73
Writer's Prop 75

PREFACE

In the spring of 2014 I was challenged to write a poem around a specific word, nemophilist. I had never written a poem, indeed I didn't think I could. But, always up to a challenge I accepted and the result is in this work. It is entitled Gisele's Place.

The title is apropos for the collection. Poems from love to war, spirituality to science, and nature to reminiscing are presented.

The first section, Love at First Voice, contains poems with the general theme of love and runs the gamut from dark endings to erotica. The next section, Bearer of Prayers, ranges from our origins to musings on the afterlife. It even has a ghost story. The section, Imagine a World, has offerings from astronomy to economics. This is followed by a group in Gisele's Place, extolling nature from a walk on a nature trail to a vista across Canada from sea to sea to sea. Lastly, in the section, Rendezvous with an Ancestor, there are poems ranging from the author's first job to his childhood chores. All are presented for your enjoyment and in that vain I hope I've succeeded.

SPECIAL THANKS

I wish to take this opportunity to thank the writers that surround me for all their encouragement. The members of Writers International Through Sarnia (WITS), especially Margaret Bird who constantly pushed me by giving the group different forms of poetry to try.

Also the members of the Lambton Writers Association many of whom have become close friends. Especially poet Debbie Okun Hill for not only encouraging me to continue writing poetry, but prodding me to join The Ontario Poetry Society along with other groups.

I also hold great appreciation for The Spoken Word, an open mic event held the last Friday of each month. It is a venue that enables new as well as old writers to read their work to an always receptive audience. Over the last year this opportunity has given me the confidence to collect the poetry I've written so far and publish them in this work. Thank you Spoken Word!

Lastly I wish to thank all my friends and relatives, especially Gisele, that I have shared my poems with for all their extolling and encouraging comments, without which this book would never have come to fruition.

Love at First Voice

Anji's Phileo

By Anjeeta Gautam, Patna, India.

*To my friend Anji whom I advise and share a brotherly love. The poem
relates our first meeting and our friendship's consequent growth. The work
is done in the first person, a one sided conversation, a monologue using her
words only and so, the issues being discussed are not fully divulged injecting a
sense of mystery to the work. A found poem and only edited slightly by myself
I consider it untreated. Phileo is one of three Greek Words for love. It means
brotherly love.*

I saw your photograph
You are the one
When I saw you the first time my heart said, yes!
Although you are far away from me, yet we are close.

The taste of emotions
The way of dealing with them, awesome!
Our words are also a wonderful way of caring
For each other.

Oh, what did you think when I first wrote to you
Why did you accept my request?
Complete strangers we were to each other
How did you decide to make me your friend?

Hello Davi, how are you?
How are you my love?
How I have been missing you
I have missed seeing you
Tell me, how are you?
Oh no! So sad, I'm getting upset!
I am praying for your good health
Come soon with your pretty smile
I am waiting and sending you my love.

How are you dear Davi?
You make me so happy to hear
You are improving each day
I love you too and wishing that you come back
As you are in yourself and enjoy your days fully.

I am missing the words that you sent me
In the early days of being my friend
I am thankful to God that without talking a lot
How we regard and care for each other

Thanks and be always with me, I love you!
You are gifted my dear friend
Your words care for me
I love you and hope we will talk more
In just a few days.

I miss you and your words
How is your health now?
You are my sweet friend and I know
From a very distance that you care for me
And thinking of me just enough
And with much love
What a gift! You are my dear friend.
I love you.

A friend like you is wonderful
I am grateful to God that he knows
Why he had made you my friend
Be healthy, wealthy and happy,
Have a long life and be with me always
And I will always smile!

I have need of your blessing, please pray for me
You are my dearest friend, be always with me
A friend forever!
It is true, the bond cannot be strong
Just between lovers

But true bonds are more and I am bound
To those for which I have no physical attraction
But I have true love with them and you are among them
I love you!

These days are my hard days
I am struggling.
I don't know when or how I will be free
Ultimately, I ask God
Why this is happening?
Well, I cannot escape
I am in a painful condition.

Can you tell me
What is love?
How do you feel for me?
Oh! You touch my heart deeply
I think you are a sweet darling
A very good spouse, father and friend. Thanks a lot dear friend
I hope the golden day will come
Hopeful I can tell my deep and hidden pains to you
Much love to you!

A happy and prosperous life to all
Live a simple but happy life
I can feel good now
Long live our friendship
Anji, with much love!

I stay myself in a relaxation
You know my marriage day is coming!
So Davi, I am a little nervous
How to manage there
But I have a little hope.

I do my domestic works and play my role
What I do is for my family so these days I am busy
Doing some works at home...
With much love, Anji

I am so happy that you will be
My mentor and spiritual adviser
It will be so good for me to have such a person
Always with me as my mentor... Thanks be to God

I like to watch you walking
But more from the front than behind
Your face dear... I just want to watch your face while walking
I'm looking at your back... Well, I like your face
Your place is a good place to be, peaceful and loving
I will come in the next life and be with you
Friends forever!

My marriage is arranged
And I am anxious until it is done!
I'm feeling not so bad now
Feeling better to this new world
In fact it's a new kind of experience
I'm so glad and happy you are with us
You are such a sweet man
Take care MY SWEET FRIEND!

Beauty

For Gisele: 'Beauty' is an acrostic poem with the subject and the title being one and the same.

Bountiful, lovely, elegance; words used to express
Exquisite beyond compare
Ardour? my love my passions abound
Utterly powerless my heart is slain
That I should succumb to your siren call
Your delicate soul has me captive, prisoner to my love for you.

Death's Sudden Embrace

'Death's Sudden Embrace' is a love sonnet that ends badly. The time is World War Two, the place is London. The young woman is a teletype operator with the Canadian Women's Army Corps at Allied Headquarters. Her lover is a fly boy who pilots a Lancaster bomber on nightly bombing runs over German occupied Europe. There were many such young women who did not know when their young men flew out at night which ones would return in the morning. And so love and life was lived day by day. This is perhaps my favourite poem. You see, the young lovers in this sonnet were my parents.

Ticker tapes ticking enhanced twenty-fold
Intel arriving bad news to behold
Blitzkrieg has started tanks roll over lines
Bombs fall on London the damn war confines

To cafes below peace can be gotten
But duty comes first success can be boughten
By lives that are lost they fly through the black
Then music and dancing the fliers are back!

That one special airman comes right on time
She lives for the daylight one day at a time
He enters the room it brightens her day
Her heart skips a beat love's funny that way
But this time he's gone, cafe's abandoned
Missing in action... His death was beckoned.

Love at First Voice

'Love at First Voice' is a simple love sonnet'. It relates an experience by the author that happened a 'long, long time ago in a galaxy far, far away'. Hearts and souls became entangled that day to remain evermore.

The phone is ringing and so I await
The pulsating stops the silence is bait
After a pause a voice... It's angelic
Her speech commences... My heart's ecstatic

My senses inform the feeling's the same
I hang up the phone I'm so glad I came
A few minutes more to see who it was
That stirred my desires I go on because

Wonder is piqued... Arrival's on time
Affairs of the heart... Arousal is mine
At last she appears and smiles just divine
Her tall slender figure... Oh she's so fine
Her long flowing locks and eyes that meet mine
Entanglement till the end of all time.

Love on the Doorstep

A cinquain with an extra line, each line ending with a word that ends in 'ing'.

She comes into view, a vision bewitching
All look up, her beauty enthralling
I've heard of her charms, her soul enchanting
She looks so awesome, her dress so stunning
She stops at my table, her smile is arresting
Dance she asks? I stand knees knocking!

Love, Murder and Madness

*A quatrain with rhyming couplets tells the fictional story of love unfulfilled,
cut short by a murderous sex crime leading to ghostly encounters and insanity.*

She worked in the bookstore
Down by the lake shore
A lovely young virgin
Innocent of sin.

Carnal knowledge she heard from
Friends who had had some
However, she kept under lock and key
Imaginings begotten by curiosity.

Then she met him, a dashing young man
Who loved her dearly and asked for her hand
He even agreed to Victorian request
To save the event till the marriage was blessed.

Darkness came early that wintry night
As she left the bookstore and locked it up tight
She cut through the park to save time in the cold
But her time was at hand and was not foretold.

The old man had watched her movements in stealth
Fixated interest precluded good health
That dark park provided the prefect crime scene
For unspeakable things, things so obscene.

Dawn's light revealed his weapon of choice
A bloody stiletto was sure to devoice
The object of his twisted desire
His undoing was about to transpire.

The old man huddled in front of his fire
Alone with his thoughts which had become dire
His mind tortured over senseless misdeeds
Intent on fulfilling tumescent needs.

Ears always hearing a most woeful sound
Clarinet providing melancholy background
For ethereal visits again and again
Drove decent into madness, no longer sane.

The jury provided the court with a verdict
Not guilty they said pronouncing the edict
Because of his mind a term with no end
Eternally haunted, to ever offend.

Of Eros and Other Things

A love sonnet of newlyweds and their wedding night.

Tell me young lovers what you discover
Erotic dance stir mingling together
Your menthol pleasure, ice coursing through veins
Together now one in both pleasure reigns

Flood tide together now come down sublime
Deep secrets revealed of love for all time
Promised forever each will concur
This moment in time stands still with ardour

Two souls speak softly those unspoken words
Of hope, faith and love raised high by halyards
Made of great purpose resolved to endure
Sacrament taken both loyal for sure
To solemn vows taken just hours before
Wedding night's bliss and excellent rapport.

Places of the Heart

My first foray into erotica! In this poem I attempt to be erotic without being graphic.

You have been where I was when
Looking in my secret places
You saw behind my lonely heart
Searching for other faces.

Oh, how I miss another soul
Entwined with mine, delightful rapture
Prodding, probing hidden recesses
Tumbling walls, secrets to capture.

Now tender couple revealing themselves
As blissful closeness, effervescent springs
Carried along by passionate current
Inner heart hears a silent bell rings.

Emotion wells from eternal fountain
Each one withdraws, then each one leads
A rhythmic timing building, building
Galloping forward on romantic steads

Becoming closer, becoming one
Forfeit identity, quickening crescendo
Mingled selves cannot distinguish
Lovers lost in dancing fandango.

Apex reached as full moon shines
Stellar flares burst like hot brilliant sun
Erotic climax. Oh, icy pleasure
All crescent now, the two become one.

Seasons of Time

This sonnet is a poem written for a very special lady for her birthday. Happy Birthday Lynn! The first stanza runs through the seasons of the year from spring to winter. The second flows backwards from winter to spring. The third reveals her character through the seasons of her life.

Royal purple crocus first to appear
Gentle breeze swaying a golden wheat's cheer
Grey skies be now descending leaves' fellow
Blankets of white sleep, but yet not callow

Seasoned by age winter's cold, icy blast
Sap's recession transport as in eons past
Sun emits fully during summer month
Preceded by spring's flowery labyrinth.

Scraped knee healing tomboy's rough play
Spring season of life is a carefree day
Now summer turns your beauty emerges
More than exemplar your soul ravishes
Through autumn carry your being so high
To winter and share God's love and grace nigh.

Bearer of Prayers

Apparition

This poem was written to extol the spirit of Halloween. It tells the story of a ghostly encounter in the Turret Room of the Lawrence House on All Hallows' Eve. Built by William Lawrence, a rich, lumber baron, in 1892 for his wife Elizabeth, the Lawrence House has remained a mainstay of ghostly encounters in Sarnia, Ontario, Canada. William died in 1922 and Elizabeth lived in the home until her death in 1940. Then the furniture was covered with sheets and the house was closed up where it remained derelict for the next four decades. It is near the end of this time the poem takes place.

He adored his love, his Elizabeth
Rich lumber baron had reached his zenith
In ninety-two he fulfilled her dreams
A two story mansion her world it seems

St. Ann's style home doted over each day
Months turn to years much to her dismay
Widow Lawrence expired wrapped in domain
Residence closed, stale air and dust claim

The decades rush on with eternal assault
Time doing its damage where once we exalt
Turning the structure to just ghostly image
Imagining visions of spectre's last vestige

Derelict gate clings to wrought iron fence
Golden rod, wild carrot growing so dense
Consuming the grounds once kept oh, so neat
Her dreams have ended, but not yet complete.

Gray skies of October set chill on the scene
While those who pass by swear they have seen
An image peer out of the top window pane
Only to vanish, no way to explain!

That night is upon us, that all-hallows eve
When fabric that parts us from phantoms unweave
And spirits walk freely among us to haunt
Their last resting places, the living to daunt

Elizabeth now can attest herself plain
To any brave soul to whom she'll explain
Why it's at night that she roams down the halls
Avoiding all doorways just passing through walls!

It's just before midnight. The brave lot arrive
A seance they'll have this psychic plus five
Mounting the staircase they climb to the top
To visit the room where she's seen quite a lot

The table is set, Turret Room is quite dim
Lit only by candle it's mood rather grim
Each manus is clasping, there's twelve hands in all
Enticing the widow, her spirit to call

Cold, deathly silence invades the room
Twelve fearless nostrils breath air filled with gloom
Suddenly power... generator kicks in
Elevator moves to the floor where within

Now tepid band awaits strange encounter
Her presence is felt, was session an error?
A more sinister cold fills the whole second floor
Extinguishing candle and they are no more!

A witness reported seeing that night
While passing the house a most frightful sight
Figures arising as faint light is quenched
Precisely at midnight, her presence now blenched.

Bearer of Prayers

A five line cinquain. In this cinquain line one contains one word for the topic, line two has two words describing the topic, line three...three words describing the action of the topic, line four...four words describing the feelings related to the topic and line five...one word that is another name for the topic.

Raptor
Magnificent bird
Soaring, diving, hunting
Noble, beautiful, stunning, awesome
Eagle

Faith, Hope and Love

'Faith, Hope and Love' is an acrostic poem about the three subjects of 1 Corinthians 13.

Fidelity in The Great Mystery
Action with principles of right
Inspire steadfast character
Toward joy and completeness
Honour, both now and evermore.

How do we stand now?
Or do we fall?
Please the one who preserves
Every day of our lives.

Let us have compassion
On one another
Viewing all with righteousness
Each one toward the other.

Immortality

This poem was inspired by the article 'Physicists Claim that Consciousness Lives in Quantum State After Death' by Janey Tracey and published in Outer Places 2015. The theory is that quantum mechanics predict some kind of 'life after death' based on an extension of wave-particle duality. Sub-atomic particles have both particle properties and wave properties at the same time with the particle writing its data on its wave function. Likewise all things have a 'quantum code' and the ability to exchange information in both directions. So this data is written on an infinite reality so when the physical is gone the consciousness lives on.

Oh my soul, my consciousness
Unfettered by time created ageless
Whence do you go when aged body dies
I know, Oh, mysteries of the synchronize

Answers lay if you're willing to dig
Sworn to secrecy yet soon to renege
The solution lay where least expected
Formerly science, the spirit rejected

Deep in the field of particle physics
Cardinal concept of quantum mechanics
Duality of particles infinitely small
Both particle and wave at once enthral

Theology of clerics tell what not how
We live immortal both future and now
A quantum code exists for all
Endlessly written upon the wall

As particle copies its data upon
Its wave this code is written hereon
In a place so small it occupies
A single dimension to internalize

Here we live forevermore
In paradigm shift we'll explore
The wonders of a new existence
We now extend without substance.

Inside My Mother's Womb

The Ojibwa Sweat Lodge Ceremony in poetic form.

At the centre of four directions
Inside my mother's womb
Where spiritual healing begins
Steam rises in grandfathers' plume

Spiritual power is given
To feminine water by cedars
Tobacco is burned a gift of prayer
Bless twenty plus eight grandfathers

Sweet grass and sage is laid
Before Creator's altar
Handled with loving care
By fire keeper and his helper

This dome-shaped lodge
It seems one door
But no, the Spirit
Sees three more

Facing east the first door's purpose
To enter and exit this sacred place
Grandfather rocks red hot allow
Steam to rise a healing grace

Drum struck four times
Eagle whistle calls
Manito helpers enter
Through spiritual walls

From each direction they come to help
Through prayer lamented
Curing soul's sickness
And songs are chanted

Each one in turn
Leaves nebulae
When all is done
All cleansed this way.

Metamorphosis

An acrostic poem describing the metamorphosis brought on by death. Not only does the first word of each line begin with each letter spelling the title vertically, so does the first letter of the last word in each line.

More than **m**utation
Ebb of life, a prescript for **e**nding
Transfigure the profane, exult in **t**ransformation
Alleviate my toilsome load **a**lways
Move away this world its barbs prick no **m**ore
Ordinance once proclaimed struggle **o**r
Refrain from death, life's import to **r**etain.
Pleasing now it seems yet to **p**ursue
Heaven's reward in warm light's **h**ue
Oh now acutely aware, sagacity bursts **o**n
Saving grace to embrace in an instant **s**ingle
Induced t'ward doxa, espoused by tepid **i**con
So it seems, but no, fond Love's **s**ubstantive.

Origins

An Ojibwa creation story in tercet poetic form.

Behold the cosmos, all that is in it
Great Mystery shaped an awesome creation
Each thing that exists, does so with spirit.

Only the human is yet to be made
But first a council, each spirit summoned
The Master of Life freeheartedly bade

Come now to reason, yes to determine
If all in accord, the species shall live
Objection brings death, less than an urchin

Consensus achieved! the spirits agree
To give of themselves, sustain the weakling
The human shall live, propped up by decree

Creator creates, environs nurture
The poor naked soul who cannot survive
Feeble in power brings only failure

Thanks are in order and so we lay down
Tobacco in prayer for love and for grace
Sacred plant given for gifts that abound.

Pain

A five line cinquain with line one containing two syllables, line two four syllables, line three six syllables, line four eight syllables and line five two syllables. Hoka comes from a Sioux saying 'Hoka Hey' said to be Crazy Horse's war cry as he rode into battle. Roughly translated to 'It's a good day to die'.

Sorrow
For lost loved one
Prayer for comfort and peace
At knowing we will meet again
Hoka!

Session on the Bench

This sonnet was inspired by meditation sessions engaged in on a park bench some 400 meters into the Osahshkedawa Wetlands. A quiet, secluded spot overlooking an L-shaped pond. A very picturesque site backed by a tall, stately white birch stand is said to be a spiritual portal and extremely easy to communicate with the Master of Life.

A lone whippoorwill its song so forlorn
The refreshing air of cool early morn
Enlivens my spirit making me well
I sit on the bench a secret I'll tell

Alone I am not as I meditate
Empty my mind to spiritual state
The spirit of God can communicate
Word manifests and my soul goes prostrate

Grace fills my being... Beyond all doubt
Our spirits embrace, a couplet devout
Tranquility comes my soul is content
Our discourse proceeds, with peace the intent
Uncertainty flees and visions they call
As frogs and song birds sing glory to all.

The Windigo from Nepissing

In Ojibwa folklore there are stories of a creature called a Windigo. These are stories of people who succumb to greed in times of hardship. Their avarice would invariably drive them to the dark arts leading them to their ultimate demise. This poem is based on one of our Windigo legends.

The winter was hard, food insufficient
The village was down to eating a fragment
Of bark for each one, their strength to recoup
Along with a cup of moccasin soup.

A young brave named Black Cloud could take it no longer
His thoughts straying constant to relief for his hunger
Now selfish concern for his famine was centric
This led him to seek relief through black magic

A magician who practised dark arts for a fee
Said he'd give him a potion to brew in a tea
He brewed the concoction and drank it all down
He knew it would work, for the doctor's renown

At once he began to grow, oh so tall
With legs, oh so long. Was this his windfall?
It could bound through drifts chest-deep or more
Outrun any deer, or chase down the boar

Over hill, over valley its long strides did carry
Black Cloud arrived overlooking my valley
While I was away on the hunt for my village
Wasn't there to observe all of the carnage.

Changing appearance, the tea was a botcher
Ribs sticking out, his skin a gray colour
It gave off a putrid, foul smelling scent
The odour of death. Down the steep hill it went

Its cries were like thunder each one a loud crack
So fearsome a sight, its monstrous attack
Some ran for their lives in timorous packs
While others so frightened fell dead in their tracks

When it arrived the village was strewn
With corpses brought down to their very ruin
The odour of death piqued its antic craving
To feast on the dead their flesh caused its binging!

Human flesh would not nourish, it only sufficed
to make it more hungry, it only enticed
To search for more dead, a most grotesque feast
To its horror it saw its famish increase!

I returned the next day to find village empty
But tell-tale signs of visit so deathly
Aghast at the sight I flew into a rage
I'd hunt the beast down where we would engage!

My weapons I gathered, set off on the hunt
To track the brute down, it will suffer the brunt
Of a fight to the death!
It will draw its last breath!

I found it along the shores of the Flint,
Where it lay exhausted, not prepared for my dint
My war club raised it plead for its life
It died very quickly without any strife.

Now this is a tale designed, yes to teach
Our youth some morals, oh I beseech!
The value that sharing has over greed
Accept now this lesson, use care, take heed!

Truth

An atheist once said that to have faith did not make a thing true. It did not even make it possibly true. That one who has faith will believe something whether it is true or not. This is my rebuttal.

Having faith it has been said
Puts not truth in to facts' stead
Nor even belike truth perceived
Fact or not will be believed.

Now this is error it's plain to see
For truth is not a noun like me
It's not a person, place or thing
That truth is fact gives hollow ring.

Truth's a verb, an action one
A way of life that teaches some
To live a life of honesty
With generous love and humility
It's faith that leads to truth, the way
Faith is truth and lives today.

Imagine a World

Thirteen Essential Literary Terms

A concrete or shape poem sometimes referred to as visual poetry. 'Thirteen Essential Literary Terms' along with examples form the shape of an umbrella signifying the covering of good writing.

Metaphor:
"She is a rose"
Simile: "She is like a rose"
Oxymoron: Military Intelligence.
Hyperbole: I have read a million books.
Irony: Saying, "How nice!" to unpleasant news.
Allegory: Jesus Christ presented as a lion in literature.
Onomatopoeia: Cuckoo, honk, boom and meow are examples.
Euphemism: The birds and the bees refers to sex and reproduction.
Allusion: She alluded to the authority of scripture to prove her point.
Alliteration: Goodness gracious great green gobs of gushy gopher guts.
Analogy: To outlaw gay marriage and inter-racial marriage is not analogical.
Satire:
To place
second
is better
than
first.
Who has
ever heard
of R1 D-1.
Paradox:
I am a   liar.
compulsive

Conundrum

This offering was inspired by a poem written by a fellow writer. The subject of the matter was philosophical in nature asking the deep questions about life to which there seems to be no definitive answers, but only speculation. Conundrum is my contribution to that speculation.

An opus I've read, profound, a just query
Racing thoughts round it makes me so weary
Provoking the mind to delve, oh so deep
Searching for truth, can make myself weep.

Is the soul an integral part of the whole?
Who leads? One of the parts or a mole?
Or is it the whole all by itself?
Singularity am I part-less myself?

Does the mystic transcend to paradise real?
Or slowly descend deceived truth will steal?
How shall I know if I'm told the truth?
Or delusional lie, I'm confused, oh forsooth!

Philosopher's ramblings how they amuse
Is it late in the night? Are they on the booze?
Theologians augustly, oh, they have spoke
But do they debate after sharing a toke?

Even musicians get in on the act
Displaying their knowledge as if it is fact
Composing their songs truth they'll rescind
"The answer my friend is blown in the wind"

Also the poet inquires with a beam
Knowing the answer is not what I deem
Asking... Is all that I see or I seem
Only a dream withheld in a dream?

This one and that one says each one can see
The truth, here it is, just listen to me
They'll come on in pairs sounding so learned
Accept now our doctrine, behold you have heard it!

The scriptures belong to the Jews so they say
The Koran revealed in Mohammad's day
The Church has her testaments both Old and New
Hindu's supreme soul and god is Vishnu

Buddha exclaims with all potency
Conjectured reality is temporary.
Sacraments some claim most decidedly
No! "Sola scriptura" others say so lordly!

Now I contribute my two cents or more
It seems we are bound by cultural lore
Some time has passed since I smoked on the matter
My search for truth drove me mad as a hatter

As interpretive beings interpret we must
Leave unknowable things to faith, which is trust
Filter all that we know through informative lens
Tis enough for the soul but the mind fails to cleanse

This answer it leaves a quandary it seems
Supra cultural knowledge taboo so She deems
On this plane we're stuck with multiple truths
To leave a conundrum for theoretical sleuths

So how should I live out my life on this earth?
To what do I measure myself to find worth?
Every thought that I have, every act that I do
If formed in agape, will find each one true.

When is it I reach the unreachable noesis?
Is the atheist right? Really? Oh no sis!
When I enter death's door at my life's conclusion
Will eternal Nirvana be just an illusion?

Imagine A World

This sonnet is a lament. It decries the replacement of the economic system of the New World with the economic system of western society.

Imagine a world if you are able
Where understanding rotates the table
Domain created, avarice unheard
Exists in history, but thought absurd
Colonial persuasion would subdue
Ideas of sharing they surely slew.

This mother earth is ours the scriptures say
God gave her to us to use in this way
We take more than we need and sell the rest
Now profit we chase to satisfy lust!

It is not our way to claim what is earned
It must be shared, have you not learned?
Your mind is corrupt, your thinking is flawed
This gainful surplus is a gift from God!

Of Quasars and Quarks

Western society sees science and spirituality as a dichotomy. The two polar opposites with many putting their faith in one or the other. 'Of Quasars and Quarks' is an attempt to meld the two by looking at the cosmos through an indigenous lens. It begins with the very large examining astrophysics then makes the quantum leap to particle physics while weaving natural theology throughout.

Night sky its beauty discovered by sight
Quasars and pulsars a show at twilight
Now clothed with twinkling points of blue light
All pushed along by dark flow's great might.

A journey so slow t'ward destiny's pain
To be reborn low and yes yet again
Implode to make colossal bright stain
Yields birth to many is this throng's refrain.

Plurality repletes a single star's nursery
Birth to some rocks who's orbs are just cursory
As galaxies swirl and dance by her bursary
Gives motion to each but struggle is tertiary.

Dark energy tends to pull us apart
And send her creation to ice cold non-start
Dark matter collapsing a plan oh so smart
A natural rebuild of sudden rampart.

Third force so quickly it moves us along
Matter through space is dark flow's sweet song
Bulge reaches in vain to touch what is wrong
Event horizon, then contact... so long!

Celestial bodies they do impress
Upon the mind a great uselessness
To search for Her in void's great starkness
Through stellar dust and black hole's darkness.

She is not there and yet She is
How can this be? A paradox tis
Will She save or send to abyss
Or create anew our place no miss.

The one we yearn for but seem without
She is within hear fabrics' tout
Newtonian physics it's not about
But photons, quarks, and strings no doubt.

Spirit resides in alternate places
Energy and matter what strange cases
For they are the same there are no spaces
A single dimension yet intricate laces.

Dimensions fold in and hadrons hold tight
While vibrating strings sing out with delight
Now darkness has fled where once there was sight
To blacken the soul and show its poor plight.

Now energy makes bright photonic flashes
Sending the spirit to embryonic masses
The spirit returns to timeless morasses
While patiently waiting the final processes.

All will be well her fabric won't fail
No matter how much the dark one might rail
Eden repeats despite his travail
When all we arrive and time it goes stale.

Gisele's Place

Aamjiwnaang

The complete meaning of the Ojibwa word Aamjiwnaang in a sonnet. Aamjiwnaang is a descriptive noun for the outlet of Lake Huron where it perpetually empties itself into the St. Clair River and its environs. The imagery in the poem represents Aamjiwnaang at the time of Confederation in 1867.

Tumbling waters tumbling by
Past boulders, and rock bed two visions vie
Thunderous falls versus mist clouds on high
Jointly both beckon to gathering nigh

Into narrow strait swift current weaves braid
Then flowing upstream beneath placid shade
In midst river yet deep deluge's not staid
Bright dancing sunbeams reveal spirits rayed

Now downstream widens it's turbulence past
Deep waters belie an irenic cast
Yet peaceful shallows raise tall reeds at last
Abode of both fish and water fowl vast
Shore boasts of maple, oak, elm all grassed
Shading wild fruit trees abundantly massed.

Gisele's Place

The author was challenged to write a poem around the word nemophilist. I had never written a poem before and had no idea I was capable. However, being the kind of person I am, always up for a challenge I accepted and 'Gisele's Place' is my first work. It is a compilation of the many walks I have done through the tall grass prairie, wetlands and woods that are on my property. The poem was fairly easy to accomplish being somewhat of a nemophilist myself. It is named in honour of my wife Gisele.

Morning dew glistens, sweet fragrance invite
Where grasses give background to splashes of white
And patches of colour reflect warm sunlight
All flowers God given for sojourn's delight.

An adventure of sorts through thicket to meadow
Among purple and oranges, red and some yellow
But green rules vista yet it is mellow
All fragrant this Eden and not very callow.

High soaring raptor, a screech is his sound
And tall aspen tremble where insects abound
Laborious ants build predominate mound
Under blossoms alive with bees' droning sound.

Gurgling spring swirls the source of a stream
That meanders to fill where water bugs teem
Amphibious song serenades their mates' gleam
While blackbird with red warbles notes of esteem.

Footsteps declare this paradise in danger!
The croaking frogs cease to avoid passing stranger
Idyllic scene soon returns with no anger
As reeds and cat tails hide motionless ranger.

So turtle returns to its sun drenched support
And heron wades feasting with oblivious retort
Encroacher moves on the trail he'll resort
To carry him forward on paths of a sort.

The entrance is guarded by stately white birch
A branch where he sits this watchful owl's perch
His wide eyes observing but he won't besmirch
His underlings stroll, his stop then his lurch.

The forest is darkened the sun's light defused
By lofty cover bright luminance refused
Where trillium and mandrake will not be abused
And Eden reclaims the path not well used.

Majestic white oak the canopy serves
Along with red maple and blue beech reserves
A spot in the sun to grow tall with no curves
Yet wind causes creaking to jangle the nerves.

The path more embellished now that it's out
Winding its way through hawthorn its route
Sharp branches protect the chickadee's tout
Scolding intruder with incessant redoubt.

On to the fen where reeds gently sway
Not from the breeze but water's the way
In the midst of a bog a lone elm will stay
To endlessly guard all it can survey.

Upon exit cow parsnip its white flowers exclaim
Don't touch or I'll burn no need to refrain
Nemophilist is a haunter he claims
of woodlands and wetlands and meadows and streams.

Ode to Canada

A lyric poem in honour of Canada's 150th birthday, July 1, 2017. A panoramic view of the country moving from sea, to sea, to sea.

Thunderous waves pound craggy shoreline
Salt water sprays high in sunshine
One lonely lighthouse stands ever to warn
Of rocky outcrop to vessels forlorn.

Sheltered harbours among infinite bays
Mullet and tern enjoy endless days
Earth's orb displays magnetic force
And tide responds with a rhythmic course.

Fresh water courses through craggy cliffs high
Preceded by rapids fed by ally
Meandering onward to ocean whereby
Whale pods play as icebergs float by.

Eager to serve they empty their lode
Ever discharging Pisces' abode
Fresh water seas tumble over great chasm
Wondrous sight, a marvel, so awesome.

Limestone escarpment crosses great distance
Spectacular vistas, ragged ridges' abundance
Petering out at Creator's great dwelling
Land of the moose where spirits are haunting.

Jewels all set in aqua blue vista
Silver sand stretches to stop the inertia
Of waves that splash upon whitened beaches
Backed by dunes sparse covered in grasses.

Thick forest canopy stretch on countless leagues
Dotted with waters until it fatigues
Sparkling in blue, dazzling like diamonds
These lakes abundant numbering thousands

Creator placed plenty in woodland's thick shelter
Bear, deer and wolf, but no numbers greater
Than industrious beaver in humble stick dome
Altering landscape with dams from his home

Now vista changes stark vision, behold!
Great plains stretch out panorama's extolled
Natural grasses wave endless it seems
Dry ocean expanse deflect golden beams

Migrating herds thunder along
Three days to pass, a colossal throng
Kicking up dust it almost smothers
Buffalo to one, bison to others.

Foothills rise gently, tectonics collide
With peaked white caps that adorn the divide
Thick timber blankets their sides so completely
To expansive salt sea they fall oh, so steeply!

Here lives the grizzly and brown bear ferocious
Sky guarded by eagle who soars ever ceaseless
Rivers that teem with chinook and sockeye
Sustaining all life with endless supply.

On northern bounds lay flora cloaked tundra
Long rivers course through spring's terra firma
Gallant elk graze as reindeer trek long
Ancient trails northward they ever belong.

Beluga and narwhal ravish flatfish buffet
Among endless ice flows where seal pups play
While warily watched over by mothers who stare
For carnivorous hunter, the white polar bear.

All through this paradise once called Kanata
The Master of Life prepared a grand schema
A bountiful land providing for all
Not one life in want there is no shortfall!

Rejuvenation

This poem was written for a friend who was experiencing a certain amount of turmoil in her life. Rather than try to give some sage advice, of which I had none, I chose to express my thoughts on the matter in this offering named 'Rejuvenation'.

Lynn, go to the garden, all care left behind
Morning's fresh air holds fragrance divined
As sun breaks horizon and meadow's dense haze
Submits to the warmth of Helios rays

Rose petals dripping dew drops to the ground
While adding perfume to the air all around
Which carries a message from one who can tell
The future is written and all will be well

Tis here we first meet where butterfly lites
With wings almost silent yet beating that writes
On the soul the same message quelling the mind
Concerns are forgotten at least for a time

While listening for content in sounds so minute
Munching of aphids, small spider astute
While riding its web as it gently sways
And hummingbirds hum while honey bee pays

For nectar it gets with feet nearly mute
Spreading its pollen and bringing forth fruit
With sounds that are drowned by city's loud bustle
And schedules and deadlines and life's busy hustle

Oh, go to the garden and seek out your balance
And listen for sounds that live in the silence
It's here that the message resounds with all calmness
Restoring the soul to its natural wellness.

The Witch of November

'The Witch of November' is a villanelle that commemorates the Great Storm that ravished the Great Lakes in November 1913. It blew from November 7th to November 10th. Its peak was on November 9th. She sank nineteen ships and claimed more than 250 lives.

Do you remember the days of November?
A wild Wiccan brew in Nineteen thirteen
The witch was born! Do you remember?

That white hurricane whose parents did whir
Like wedding dance twirled, a king and queen
Do you remember the days of November?

Clipper and low churned waves out in anger
From crest to trough three stories between
The witch was born! Do you remember?

All good men sailed smooth in September
Found watery graves that day all unseen
Do you remember the days of November?

November Gale its colour was amber
Freshwater Fury lash beaches obscene
The witch was born! Do you remember?

Big Blow blew four days low pressure's daughter
Big ships like toy boats capsized unforeseen
Do you remember the days of November?
The witch was born! Do you remember?

Wihat, Tico and Bear

A standard acrostic poem, but with the last letter in the last word of each line spelling the title when read vertically. Wihat and Tico are the author's two Chihuahuas and Bear his Mastiff. The three often travel the nature trail through the tall grass prairie and woods together. This poem describes an imaginary confrontation with a coyote on the trail.

Wihat, Tico and Bear in to**w?**
It seems two with courage as thistle's papp**i**
Happily followed by defender large enoug**h**
A Mastiff named Bear causing great phobi**a**
This giant behemoth, yet gentle sugges**t**

Till danger appears to each yappy to**t**
Into action he springs this powerful mag**i**
Crushing the adversary, intimidating tacti**c**
Onward three march, the vanquished left blott**o**

Arrear the threat soothes injured aur**a**
Never to assail these three agai**n**
Doubtless Bear is king of wood and fiel**d**

Bear and Wihat and Tico, nay bo**b!**
Ever three comrades in arms they ar**e**
And if two Chihuahuas come upon your are**a**
Retreat to safety for they have a staunch protecto**r.**

Rendezvous with an Ancestor

Cold Winter Chores

A day in the life of the author circa 1954. Dead of winter chores: it was my duty to arise from my unheated, but insulated attic bedroom first, get a fire going in the kitchen and re-stoke the coal furnace in the cellar so the home would be comfortably warm for parents and siblings when they arose. I loved this job not only because it made me feel useful, but it also taught me the value of doing something for others.

The kitchen is heated by coal burning chamber
A brick is warmed in the kiln so tender
The burners and oven are natural gas
But this breathless comrade's warmth won't last.

Jack Benny has bid Rochester good night
Mantle clock chimed, nine times it is right
For boy to bunk in for a long winter's night
Where breath can be seen in pale moonlight

Up attic staircase boy trudges alone
A cordless heating pad his very own
Hot brick in flannel to help keep him warm
At least for a time till cold overwhelms

Numerous blankets help keep him in place
Snug in his bed his dreams to embrace
While fires die down and cold overtakes
The warmth of the home, then morning breaks.

Twilight breaks through frosted panes to awake
The lad to his chores, frigid floors that await
The warming that comes with new fires stoked
By the youth who prepares a welcome evoked

Down staircase he's nimble, cold hot-pad in tow
Cook stove's coal chamber is first to bestow
A welcoming heat from logs that were split
A mercury reverse after kindling's been lit

The boy and his bucket tread down cellar stairs
Where slumbering behemoth has lost all its cares
If octopus left its purpose just dies
But boy pokes and prods causing sparks to arise

Old ogre awakes raising its hackles
Hungry for fuel this monster that crackles
Gaping mouth ready the boy will oblige
With shovels of coal, the giant subsides

Iron door closed with black smoke locked in
Jacket replenished holds water within
Now refill the bucket, haul coal up the stairs
Replenish the chamber so each fire flares

Warming the home with a welcoming warmth
The kitchen's now toasty a comforting wealth
The boy's tepid greeting to his family's delight
He now feels worthy, his chores made it right.

Dammit I'm Mad

An acrostic poem based on the palindrome 'Dammit I'm Mad' as a response to comments to an article about the Truth and Reconciliation Commission Report on residential schools in Canada.

Don't you know, can't you see
An iota of decent sense does flee
More a thread of wilful bliss
Mostly ignorance shown as this
In comment, replies no not me
Those deeds were done by others they plea.

In other lands, another time
Most genocides were worse they chime

Most genocides were worse I ask?
At first glance that's not the task
Do not in moral smugness bask!

Growing Old

A Kyrielle poem, a French form, written in rhyming quatrains with the last line a refrain. It reveals some of the authors feelings on growing old.

Sometimes I try my very best
To grasp things lost. I need some rest
I have no gas. I cannot last.
There seems no way to claim the past!

Once toned muscle has turned to flab
A heavy load at first I'll grab.
Can't lift it now, the die is cast
There seems no way to claim the past!

My joints ache. It's not the flu.
Now pills and drops to get me through.
The end is near, it's coming fast.
There seems no way to claim the past!

Into the room with goal in mind
When I get there I am resigned
Forgetfulness. I am aghast!
There seems no way to claim the past!

A pretty girl, oh my, she's fine.
When I walk by she gives no sign.
I'm not noticed. I am outcast.
There seems no way to claim the past!

Party all night I used to do.
Booze flowed freely, good times too.
A screeching halt that came so fast.
There seems no way to claim the past!

I'd taken breaths two score and ten.
The surgeons knife would cut me then.
Twice more since first, also a cast.
There seems no way to claim the past!

I'm giving up on going back.
I will concede. I'll give no flack.
Life's past me by. I've been surpassed.
There seems no way to claim the past!

I'm so sorry for ranting on.
So hard done by...time moves along.
I will accept, but am downcast.
There seems no way to claim the past!

But things are not so bad at all.
There is no clock or boss to call
A few choice names...he can't lambast.
There seems no way to claim the past!

There's steady income coming in
For forty years of toil for him.
It is enough that I've amassed.
There seems no way to claim the past!

My time's my own, do what I please
And so I write with pleasure's ease
Books and poems till I'm bedfast.
There seems no way to claim the past!

The future's bright long term, kaput
When coins upon my eyes are put.
I'll float into that light so vast.
There seems no way to claim the past!

Limericks in Honour of John

I wrote these three limericks in honour of my friend, John Drage, whose limericks, humour and wit was renowned in Lambton County.

I once knew a man named Drage
Whose humour was said rather strange
John's wit rather dry, his verse oh so sly
From smile to laughter his range!

There once was a man named John
Whose humour will surely live on
His wit all the rage, this man called John Drage
A legend in time and beyond!

I once heard a limerick by John
Whose verses went on and on
My attention was captured, my interest was raptured
What humour John Drage would adorn!

Remember the Raisin

*On the 21st of January 1813 Colonel Henry Proctor's force was passed by
the Wyandotte War Chiefs Roundhead and Splitlog's warriors on snowshoes
gliding over the deep snow drifts covering Hull's road between Detroit
and Frenchtown. The Americans were advised but chose to discount the
intelligence not believing they would make such a trek in the dead of winter.
The battle was lost by the Americans and their sick and wounded were left
lightly guarded by Proctor. When they complained he is said to have replied,
'The Indians make excellent doctors.'*

The news had reached Malden, and it was not good!
Big Knives took Frenchtown, it had not stood
His troops have fled, the post it has fallen
Best raise the allies to come a-callin.

Muster the men to cross the de troit
Over thick ice his plan was adroit
Through knee deep snow his men would trudge
To catch Hull's trail, snow drifts would grudge.

Roundhead and Split Log sent the war belt
To nations encamped near Malden for help
By raising war parties of men oh, so brave
Hundreds of warriors, it's vengeance they crave.

For atrocities done last autumn it's said
To women and children and even the dead.
Blackbird and Bluejacket smudge then they do
Don their wide snowshoes and hand weapons too!

Proctor and band they soon overtook
The soldiers would stop to take second look,
Men feathered and painted and in buckskin frills
With hair greased high like porcupine quills

Armed to the teeth intent on the business
Of battle with bravery not one was spineless
They reached River Raisin hours ahead
Of six hundred Redcoats through deep snow they tread

Dragging their cannon through drifts near hip deep
Six pounders on sleighs their progress did creep
Till finally arriving just before dawn
Artillery facing Frenchtown head on

Winchester was there with Lewis and men
Numbering one hundred brave souls times ten
All settled in for a long winter's wait
Expecting no fight from the enemy's gate

John Baptiste Askin and his Essex Militia
Put Raisin's small town in a kind of dilemma
By joining with Splitlog to aggress from the west
But Madison held and they could not best

Even though Walk-In-The-Water was there
Along with old Bluejacket brought pressure to bear
But the left side did crumble and panic set in
They flung down their arms in the midst of the din

The big guns had boomed blowing holes in defence
But Proctor had placed them in front of offence
Exposing his gunners to crossfire it seems
Although he was censured not ending his dreams.

Big Knives they scrambled across frozen stream
Led by Winchester who would only mean
To save what he could of his men but in vain
Because of his capture but Roundhead would deign

To give him his death the honourable way
But dragged him to Proctor alive he would stay
To sign Proctor's order Kentucky would cave
The battle now done, the braves misbehave.

The loot's biggest prize was liquor not milk
Fuelling harsh hatred for Yanks and their ilk
Disdain for Ken tuck raging within
It spilled out to action causing great sin

The sick and the wounded tomahawked on the spot
Or shot or else stabbed then scalped by the lot
The British would give them no help from abrasion
Giving rise to the call, 'Remember the Raisin!'

Rendezvous with an Ancestor

This poem consists of rhyming couplets describing a memory. It remembers a hot summer's day, an approaching thunder storm and an old man. The old man is my grandfather who enjoyed nothing more in his old age than a good cigar and a visit from his great-great grandfather. Nimikiins or Little Thunder was an Ojibwa War Chief who visited us often on those hot summer afternoons. There was nothing I enjoyed more as a boy than to sit with him on that veranda on Exmouth Street and take in Nimikiins' awesome power.

Searing sun beats down on asphalt
Too hot to tread the feet does assault
Hot weather calls for shorts and tank top
And lone robin chirps for nature's raindrop

Hot stagnant air harms cool breeze belief
But shade covered porch provides some relief
Gentle warm air washes over the face
And rustles the leaves high in their place

Spring loaded screen door slams shut behind
Old man on bowed legs shuffles to find
His favourite seat on rocker his choice
He'll sit in silence, he'll add no voice

He takes out cigar his favourite pass-time
To smoke on his thoughts of past paradigms
He strikes Eddy's match, he draws on White Owl
As robin awaits a response to its call

Ominous clouds the horizon's hedge
Flashes alight dark billow's edge
Tempest approaches but not quick enough
While quivering lips draw uneasy puff.

Soon deluge cools hot pavement's breath
By droplets that bounce... Oh, inches at best
Hot summer breeze turns cool season's wind
Strong maple bends but comes not unpinned

Dark sky alights with electric display
Ozone's burnt odour drives robin away
Thunderous cracks produced the scent
Repeats and repeats until it is spent

Storm travels eastward enabling blue sky
Above cooled pavement steam rises high
Robin returns to hop all about
Then tugs on a worm the rain has coaxed out

The old man relights content at his visit
Nimikiins returned his power's implicit
To visit descendant and relive the time
When enemies quaked at this warrior's prime.

Summer in the City

A sonnet celebrating a few of the many cultural events held during the summer in the City of Sarnia, Ontario, Canada.

Sparkling blue waters lap sandy shore
Of lake and river and yes there is more
White sails dot expansive horizon
While freighter's pilot acts as a lineman.

Green parks afford our cultural events
ArtWalk with crafts under colourful tents
Artists with oils, musicians play loud
Food vendors offer their wares to the crowd.

First Friday appears as each month begins
Galleries, cafes and shops greet with grins
Citizens with guests, the populace wins!

Drumming and dancing each June can be found
With singing while vendors ply powwow ground
Fortunate Sarnians! Blessings abound!

The Keys to the Kingdom

The Bop is a poetic form developed by poet Alfaa Michael. It has three stanzas each followed by a refrain. The first stanza has six lines, the second eight and the third six for a total of twenty-three lines. The first stanza outlines a problem. The second expands on it and the third records success or failure. The poem recalls a period of my youth spent picking losers at the racetrack.

Off to the track
That mysterious place
Where fortunes are sought
By foretelling the future
Win, place or show
Exotic wager, now that is the ticket.

The Keys to the Kingdom you passionately pursue!

With form in hand
Astutely you study
The mysterious symbols
Each line contains
Looking for Breaks
And trials that fit
That tell if the steed
Comes to form or retreats.

The Keys to the Kingdom you passionately pursue!

Purchase your tickets your selection to pay
Double or triple your wager or more!
Exactas, Trifactas or maybe you'll pick
The big one, Superfecta that's seven in a row!
Now it is over the floor littered with losers
A new dawn arises with a chance yet again

The Keys to the Kingdom you passionately pursue!

The Very Best Years

This poem relates some of the author's highlights in life. Somewhat humourous it is a reflection of my thoughts as I look back at events. I did crash and burn a couple of times, but I chose to leave those times out.

Commencement, a time of excellent rapport
When spheres expand with good friends galore
Collegians supply a very large clique
While Brylcreem holds down a stubborn cowlick

Long summer days on hot summer sands
Sock hops and band shells with rock and roll bands
Pushing the wrapper this side of heaven
Glory days turn in year fifty-seven.

Into the sixties, hot nights, cool times
Fast cars and hot chicks alter good minds
Testing the night clubs with doctored I.D.
Yet I would fall in year sixty-three.

Multinational has hired and given a chance
For technical skills to do a grand dance
Fortran and binary math at the core
Languages used in seventy-four.

Still youthful a man at age thirty-five
Rejoining the rat race to prove I'm alive
Dances and parties and partners... I'm free!
Oh, trapped again! It's now eighty-three.

Sneakily sneaking she snuck up like a sneak
While studying deep thought of scholastic God speak
Midterm overtook this body of mine
The nineties arrive, it's year ninety-nine!

Calling again those church bells did ring
I'll try yet again, matrimonious thing
Write a few books before I see heaven
A decade slips by, it's now year aught seven.

Producer arrives with a deal in line
A series based on a novel of mine
Contract is signed, but the end is unseen
Old age is here it's now year fifteen.

How all will end I really can't say
Don't know when I'll die, though not yet I pray
This poem's not done nor finally read
Ode should be finished on author's death bed!

Wafting

Two acrostic poems about Thanksgiving and the wafting aromas that holiday effects. The first one is a prose poem and the second a rhyming poem.

What is it? This scent that tickles the nostrils
Airwaves a carrier, appetites piqued
First thing that slaps the guest at the door
Turkey n' dressing baste, while pumpkin pies cool
Into the oven an all day roast, gravy is made
Never late, potatoes are mashed, squash is squished
Grace is said, the family, at last - digs in!

When grey skies force the chill of November
And the pumpkin's ripe, do you remember?
For old time's sake, the family gathering
Third Thursday's table, most formal setting
Intriguing aromas filling the room
Now memory of Aunt Bess arriving on broom
Grand entry she makes, so we will feast soon!

Worm Pickers' Delight

A poem reminiscing about a lesson learned during those days between adolescence and adulthood. A time when I was most desperate to grow up, get a job, my own place and support myself. Oh, and a car. I needed a car! But sixteen was not the age that these things would come.

"Worm Pickers Wanted"... Gave phone number only
The classified said, and said rather pronely.
The youth was searching desperate to find
Employment to help him out of a bind.

He needed a job to help with the rent
Lest he be moving from room to a tent
So he picked up the phone and dialed the number
Although the position was just for the summer.

"Come on right down!"... That thickened the plot.
He did right away... Was hired on the spot.
The motley crew scrambled into the van
None could speak English. The adventure began.

Elastic bands strapped tin cans to his ankles
So tightly they hold.... Oh how it rankles!
The lantern was strapped tight to his head
He's ready for work but what lies ahead?

Soon they arrived at work's destination
He scarcely could stand the anticipation!
Cube van's back door swung open to view
The job site's expansive, outside his purview.

A golf course it seems is where he would work
All through the night his sore arms would jerk
Like a chicken he's pecking the ground all around
Picking up worms from greens, they're fogbound

The back it is bent from dusk until dawn
While filling those cans with worms off the lawn
He wished the damn night wasn't so long
If only the rent could be paid with a song.

After suffering weeks of this horrible torture
While nothing was done to increase his stature.
Convinced that his back was eternally bent
Being paid by the can barely covered the rent.

So he thought of a plan to escape the long anguish
No longer he thought will he toil, will he languish
To college he'll go and get a degree!
Back to his parents and give them the plea

He'd learned his lesson and the heart of the matter
Life's really the pits at the end of the ladder
Education's the answer... A career after college!
They welcomed him home secure in the knowledge

He'd try even harder receiving good grades
Make his mark in this world... Success and in spades!
He's old now, retired and looks back on his life
Knowing all that he owes to that horrible strife

'Worm Pickers Wanted' how those words blessed
A lesson in life. Who would have guessed?
A valuable teaching from a job such a fright
On that golf course they called 'Worm Pickers' Delight'.

Writer's Prop

A sonnet about coffee without using the words coffee, beans, black, milky, cafe or caffeine.

Wafting aroma pry open one's eyes
To greet morning light the ocular lyse?
REM sleep, so it flees to shadowy night
Deep brewed fragrance gives pleasant invite

Timer preset auto maker for seven
Rise and prepare that first cup of heaven
Arabian dark a drug most preferred
Scribe samples before uttering a word

A second cup prompts, workday to begin
Neurons are firing as ideas unpin
The writer she writes, the poet he pens
Of lovely green glens, of darkened still fens.
The stimulant flows as day hurries by
Last cup now savoured, day ends with a sigh.

Printed in the United States
By Bookmasters